Reading Between the Lines
Drawing correct inferences

Walter Pauk, Ph.D.
Professor of Education
Director, Reading-Study Center
Cornell University

Jamestown Publishers
Providence, Rhode Island

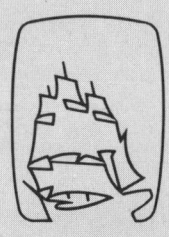

A Skill at a Time Series
   No. ST-5 Reading Between the Lines

ISBN 0-89061-025-8

Copyright © 1975 by Jamestown Publishers, Inc.

All rights reserved. The original material contained in this book is protected under the United States Copyright Law. It is illegal to copy or reproduce any pages or parts of any pages. Address inquiries to Editor, Jamestown Publishers, Post Office Box 6743, Providence, Rhode Island 02940.

Cover and Text Design by
Stephen R. Anthony

Printed in the United States

CONTENTS Preface 4

To Students 5

Reading Between the Lines 9

A Skill at a Time Paragraphs 13

Answer Key & Recording Chart 64

PREFACE For anyone who wants to improve his basic reading skills, there is no truer, nor surer advice than: "Well, begin *reading*." Read words, signs, labels, short stories, books . . . but *read*! In other words, *practice, practice, practice.*

This is good and sufficient advice for developing the basic skills needed for reading labels and straightforward writing. But when it comes to reading mature writing, then this kind of undirected, trial-and-error practice has serious limitations.

Without directed practice, it is easy to imagine a person going through life almost totally unaware, for example, of the value of *signal words,* of the symbolic meaning of *figurative* language, of how to recognize *points of view,* and so forth. To save students from falling into such a serious "reading gap," this series of books was written.

This series of ten books is an outgrowth of notions, ideas and insights gathered over a period of more than twenty years. And during this time, many of these notions, ideas and insights were honed and polished in classes and seminars at Cornell, and thereby and therein they emerged as the ten essential categories which now form the basis for this practical and systematic program.

And now to acknowledge gladly my debts: To those students who took part in my classes and seminars, I give thanks for I learned much from them. My especial thanks goes to those students who contributed or suggested some unusually good excerpts to add to the store I already had.

In addition, I wish cordially to thank Jean Cahill of the English Department of the Providence Public Schools for her part in polishing and refining the questions.

And finally, thanks to G. Edward Lewis, Chairman, Humanities Department at Mt. Pleasant Area Senior High School in Westmoreland County, Pennsylvania, for reading all of the introductory lessons in these texts and improving them in many ways. And to all others, too numerous to mention, who have helped, I thank and am forever indebted.

Walter Pauk

Ithaca, New York
1975

TO STUDENTS   When you say, "Let me get my hands on it," you are in harmony with the number one principle of all education: *Learning by doing.* All educators know this principle, and they use it. That's why we have labs in accounting, woodworking, chemistry, and so forth.

And that's why this book was necessary. It was necessary to provide a *personal lab* so you could get your hands and mind on actual material.

But, to make this material really useful, we still needed to get *concentration* on our side. And fortunately we were able to do so. We did it by devising the one-skill-at-a-time technique.

So finally, a fully balanced program emerged. We combined a powerful principle with a powerful technique to give us a personal lab of 100 exercises. Now you will be able to focus your attention on mastering one skill before moving on to another. Your concentration will not be jarred by the mixed-question approach. You won't be forced to shift your concentration from one type of question to another.

Scanning for Author and Title   Edward Gibbon, the great historian who wrote the *Decline and Fall of the Roman Empire*, always used it. He would take a few minutes to recall what he already knew about the author and the story. Even the smallest bit of information would establish in his mind a "magnetic center" around which would cluster, like iron filings, the events of the story.

You, too, can use scanning not only for establishing magnetic centers, but also for gaining instant concentration. Once you establish a *mental set* on the story, it is difficult for outside thoughts to break in. So, with concentration and magnetic centers on your side, comprehension of a high level is bound to result.

Using the Gestalt-Dot System   *Gestalt* is a German word meaning "the whole thing." So, Gestalt psychologists would say, "Read the whole passage to get an immediate overall idea. Then go back to read each sentence more carefully. Now each sentence will be understood in relation to the whole."

To develop this concept into a useful skill, make the Gestalt sweep first, and on the basis of this first reading, answer the question by placing a dot in the square beside the option that you think is correct. This dot will indicate your unofficial answer.

Using the Check-Mark System

Now, re-read the passage, but this time indicate your official answer with a check mark (✓). This answer will count toward your final score.

The Optimum Learning Bite

The optimum learning bite is five passages. So, after every five passages, transfer your official answers to the lower portion of each block of the Answer Key Chart. The upper portion of each block already contains the correct answer. So, if your answer is correct, make no additional mark. But, if your answer is incorrect, then circle it. With your incorrect answers thus identified, take the next step.

Taking Corrective Action

Your incorrect answers provide an opportunity to continue the process of self-learning. Now that you know the correct answer, re-read the passage to see why the approved option is correct and analyze why you chose the incorrect option.

Recording Your Score

Tear out the Answer Key Chart page. Having the sheet in front of you will make it easier to record your official answers and to refer to it as your eyes check back and forth during the correction stage. Give yourself twenty points for each correct answer.

The Steps in a Nutshell

1. *Author-Title Scanning:* Spend a minute to recall what you know about both. This recall establishes powerful "magnetic centers," as well as instant concentration.
2. *The Gestalt-Dot System:* Read the passage straight through to grasp the big picture, then answer the question using the unofficial dot.
3. *The Check-Mark System:* Re-read the passage carefully. This time, put a check mark (✓) in a block to indicate your official answer.
4. *The Optimum Learning Bite:* After completing five passages, stop to check your answers.
5. *The Answer Key Chart:* Transfer your official answers to the Answer Key Chart. Circle the incorrect ones.
6. *Corrective Action:* Investigate all incorrect answers. Analyze your mistakes.
7. *Record Your Score:* Record your comprehension score.

READING BETWEEN THE LINES

READING BETWEEN THE LINES

Has someone ever said something to you that made you stop and think: "Did he mean this or that?" At that precise moment you were trying to "read between the lines," trying to grasp the entire meaning of the comment. Reading between the lines is another way of saying that there is more meaning intended than what has been stated or written. And, therein lies the key to being able to "read between the lines." One can develop the ability to read for the stated (denoted) meaning. However, one also can develop the ability to read for the unstated or implied (connoted) meaning.

Implication Versus Inference

An author often *implies* his real meaning. It then becomes the reader's task to uncover and capture the full strength of the implication. When a person does understand all that is happening, he *infers* his real or underlying meaning.

In this excerpt from "God Sees the Truth, But Waits to Tell," Leo Tolstoy implies a meaning, Aksenov has been sent to prison for killing a man. However, he did not kill the man at all, and while he is in prison he discovers the man who did. Here is that passage.

> (Makar Semenov said) But how could anyone have shoved a knife into your bag? Was it not at your bed-head? You would have heard him.
>
> As soon as Aksenov heard these words he thought within himself that this was the very man who killed the merchant.

How did Aksenov know this? What implication or clue does Tolstoy provide? If you picked the bed-head, you're right. But then the passage goes on.

> And such a bitterness against Makar Semenov came upon him that he longed to be avenged upon him though it were to his own destruction. He recited prayers all night, but he found no rest for his soul. In the daytime he did not go near to Makar Semenov nor even look at him. Aksenov could not sleep at nights, and such a weary longing came over him that he knew not what to do with himself. Thus three weeks passed away.

This example is clearly written, but Tolstoy is implying more than he has written. What kind of man is Aksenov, the innocent? What kind of man is Makar, the real killer? Why can't Aksenov sleep at night? What is gnawing away inside him? Is Tolstoy trying to tell us that Aksenov has set himself up as a judge? The poor man is so desirous of revenge that he is letting it poison him. He avoids the real killer and, in that way, is not loving his enemies — a way of life that he always embraced. Thus, he too becomes as bad as the killer for he desires the killer's death.

We must infer that Tolstoy is placing faith in God. He seems to be saying that all people will get their just rewards in the end, and men should not take it upon themselves to play God and wish for another's death or punishment. We must recognize Tolstoy's implication that man is man, and man should not wish to be more than man — that love is more powerful than hate.

An Inference Is More Than a Guess

To be sure, your inferences must not be simply guesses. An author has planned his story. Learn to base your inferences on his choice of words, on his logic and sequence, and on the focus or purpose of the story. This takes practice, and even experts make mistaken inferences at times. An author implies something by hinting; we must base our inferences on those hints.

Inference Versus Assumption

It is also desirable to distinguish between inference and assumption. An inference is a logical conclusion based on hints that are stated or implied. An assumption is usually a conclusion that has been leaped to without really having the proof or facts to back it up. Consider this passage from William Dean Howells's "Editha." Editha has convinced her boyfriend that he should volunteer to go to war even though he does not want to. This is part of a conversation that followed his signing-up:

> Editha: "That's all past. I've been thinking and worshipping *you*. Don't you suppose I know all you've been through to come to this? . . . And I know you've done it from the highest motives — And you haven't simply done it for my sake. I couldn't respect you if you had."
>
> George: "Well, then say I haven't. A man that hasn't got his

own respect intact wants the respect of all the other people he can corner. But we won't go into that . . . . If anything happens to me —"

"Oh George!" She clung to him, sobbing.

"I don't want you to feel foolishly bound to my memory . . . ."

"I am yours, for time and eternity — time and eternity." She liked the words; they satisfied her famine for phrases.

To make the assumption that Editha is realistic or right — that George has made up his own mind and is not just going off to war to please her — would be inconsistent with the rest of the story. However, because they are in love and because Editha can spout pretty phrases like being his for all eternity, some readers might leap to her side, might see her as a heroine. A more careful reader might infer, instead, that Editha is a pithy girl who is quite happy to just mouth slogans without following through with real actions. It is easy to say that a citizen has a duty to defend his country as long as you, yourself, are not marching off to battle. Editha is young and idealistic, and she has forced this man to do something he does not believe in because he fears losing her love. These kinds of interpretations are supported by the story's development; the earlier assumption is not.

In Summary The process of inferring may seem difficult at first because it requires an intuitive leap. But once you become accustomed to arranging the facts and hints before you, inferring will follow easily. Begin with the title of the story for practice. From a simple title such as Shirley Jackson's "The Lottery," you can infer that someone or something is going to win and someone or something else is going to lose. Read the story and see if I'm right. With this kind of practice and the knowledge that inferences must be based on the full context of a passage, you soon will find yourself grasping meanings that go far beyond the written words!

THE ADVENTURES OF TOM SAWYER
Mark Twain
1

The boys bent their heads together and scarcely breathed. A muffled sound of voices floated up from the far end of the graveyard.

"Look! See there!" whispered Tom. "What is it?"

"It's devil-fire. Oh, Tom, this is awful."

Some vague figures approached through the gloom, swinging an old-fashioned tin lantern that freckled the ground with innumerable little spangles of light. Presently Huckleberry whispered with a shudder:

"It's the devils, sure enough. Three of 'em! Lordy, Tom, we're goners! Can you pray?"

"I'll try, but don't you be afeard. They ain't going to hurt us. Now I lay me down to sleep, I—"

The fact that they are in a graveyard at night, one might infer that Tom and Huckleberry are
☐ a. running away from home.
☐ b. an adventure loving duo.
☐ c. visiting the grave of a loved one.
☐ d. the victims of foul play.

ROBINSON CRUSOE
Daniel Defoe
2

I was perfectly confounded at the sight, and knew not what the meaning of it should be. Friday called out to me in English as well as he could, "O master! you see English mans eat prisoner as well as savage mans." "Why," says I, "Friday, do you think they are a-going to eat them then?" "Yes," says Friday, "they will eat them." "No, no," says I, "Friday, I am afraid they will murder them indeed, but you may be sure they will not eat them."

It may be clearly inferred from this paragraph that
☐ a. Friday was not an Englishman.
☐ b. Englishmen are superior to savages.
☐ c. Friday likes to eat human flesh.
☐ d. Englishmen are absolutely reasonable.

UP FROM SLAVERY
Booker T. Washington
3

During the time that I was a student at Hampton my older brother, John, not only assisted me all that he could, but worked all of the time in the coal-mines in order to support the family. He willingly neglected his own education that he might help me. It was my earnest wish to help him to prepare to enter Hampton, and to save enough money to assist him in his expenses there.

This man's feelings toward his brother were
☐ a. antagonistic.
☐ b. pitying.
☐ c. appreciative.
☐ d. confused.

THE WIND IN THE WILLOWS
Kenneth Grahame
4

"You know it must come to this, sooner or later, Toad," the Badger explained severely. "You've disregarded all the warnings we've given you, you've gone on squandering the money your father left you, and you're getting us animals a bad name in the district by your furious driving and your smashes and your rows with the police. Independence is all very well, but we animals never allow our friends to make fools of themselves beyond a certain limit; and that limit you've reached. Now, you're a good fellow in many respects, and I don't want to be too hard on you. I'll make one more effort to bring you to reason. You will come with me into the smoking-room, and there you will hear some facts about yourself; and we'll see whether you come out of that room the same Toad that you went in."

The Badger implies that the Toad is
☐ a. young.
☐ b. capable.
☐ c. irresponsible.
☐ d. sad.

CHARLOTTE'S WEB
E. B. White
5

"I'm staying right here," grumbled the rat. "I haven't the slightest interest in fairs."

"That's because you've never been to one," remarked the old sheep. "A fair is a rat's paradise. Everybody spills food at a fair. A rat can creep out late at night and have a feast. In the horse barn you will find oats that the trotters and pacers have spilled. In the trampled grass of the infield you will find old discarded lunch boxes containing the foul remains of peanut butter sandwiches, hard-boiled eggs, cracker crumbs, bits of doughnuts, and particles of cheese . . . . Everywhere is loot for a rat, in tents, in booths, in hay lofts—why, a fair has enough disgusting left-over food to satisfy a whole army of rats."

The speaker knew that the
☐ a. rat really wanted to go to the fair.
☐ b. way to a rat's heart is through his stomach.
☐ c. fair grounds would be in tidy condition.
☐ d. fair-goers would welcome a rat's presence.

THE ADVENTURES OF TOM SAWYER
Mark Twain
6

Tom appeared on the sidewalk with a bucket of whitewash and a long-handled brush. He surveyed the fence, and all gladness left him and a deep melancholy settled down upon his spirit. Thirty yards of board fence nine feet high. Life to him seemed hollow, and existence but a burden. Sighing he dipped his brush and passed it along the topmost plank; repeated the operation; did it again; compared the insignificant whitewashed streak with the far-reaching continent of unwhitewashed fence, and sat down on a tree-box discouraged.

Tom sat down discouraged because he
☐ a. had the wrong color paint.
☐ b. didn't know how to paint.
☐ c. didn't want to do the job.
☐ d. was afraid of heights.

UP FROM SLAVERY
Booker T. Washington
7

In order to be successful in any kind of undertaking, I think the main thing is for one to grow to the point where he completely forgets himself; that is, to lose himself in a great cause. In proportion as one loses himself in this way, in the same degree does he get the highest happiness out of his work.

From this passage, one can infer that the author is
☐ a. ambitious.
☐ b. foolhardy.
☐ c. dedicated.
☐ d. lazy.

THE WIND IN THE WILLOWS
Kenneth Grahame
8

... "Ho, ho!" he said to himself as he marched along with his chin in the air, "what a clever Toad I am! There is surely no animal equal to me for cleverness in the whole world! My enemies shut me up in prison, encircled by sentries, watched night and day by warders; I walk out through them all, by sheer ability coupled with courage. They pursue me with engines, and policemen, and revolvers; I snap my fingers at them, and vanish, laughing, into space. I am, unfortunately, thrown into a canal by a woman fat of body and very evil-minded. What of it? I swim ashore, I seize her horse, I ride off in triumph, and I sell the horse for a whole pocketful of money and an excellent breakfast! Ho, ho! I am The Toad, the handsome, the popular, the successful Toad!"

An obvious conclusion is that the Toad is
☐ a. contemptuous of himself.
☐ b. ashamed of himself.
☐ c. pleased with himself.
☐ d. worried about himself.

TREASURE ISLAND
Robert Louis Stevenson
9

In one way, indeed, he bade fair to ruin us; for he kept on staying week after week, and at last month after month, so that all the money had been long exhausted, and still my father never plucked up the heart to insist on having more. If ever he mentioned it, the captain blew through his nose so loudly that you might say he roared, and stared my poor father out of the room. I have seen him wringing his hands after such a rebuff, and I am sure the annoyance and the terror he lived in must have greatly hastened his early and unhappy death.

One can readily determine that the father was a
☐ a. happy-go-lucky type.
☐ b. fearless man.
☐ c. wealthy man.
☐ d. timid man.

THE ADVENTURES OF TOM SAWYER
Mark Twain
10

"Huckleberry, what do you reckon'll come of this?"
"If Dr. Robinson dies, I reckon hang'll come of it."
"Why, I know it, Tom."
Tom thought a while, then he said:
"Who'll tell? We?"
"What are you talking about? S'pose something happened and Injun Joe didn't hang? Why, he'd kill us some time or other, just as dead sure as we're lying here."

From this passage, we can conclude that Huck and Tom
☐ a. saw Injun Joe try to kill Dr. Robinson.
☐ b. helped Injun Joe kill Dr. Robinson.
☐ c. watched Injun Joe murder Dr. Robinson.
☐ d. were good friends of Injun Joe.

17

THE GOLDEN HONEYMOON
Ring Lardner
11

We seen the Hartsells the next day in the Park and I was willing to apologize, but they just nodded to us. And a couple of days later we heard they had left for Orlando, where they have got relatives.

I wish they had went there in the first place.

The passage definitely indicates that the Hartsells
☐ a. were close friends of the speaker.
☐ b. lived in Orlando.
☐ c. were not liked by the speaker.
☐ d. would accept an apology.

THE ADVENTURES OF TOM SAWYER
Mark Twain
12

At half past nine, that night, Tom and Sid were sent to bed, as usual. They said their prayers, and Sid was soon asleep. Tom lay awake and waited, in restless impatience. When it seemed to him that it must be nearly daylight, he heard the clock strike ten! This was despair. He would have tossed and fidgeted, as his nerves demanded, but he was afraid he might wake Sid. So he lay still, and stared up into the dark.

One might suppose, from the above passage, that Tom
☐ a. didn't feel well.
☐ b. had plans for the morning.
☐ c. was nervous.
☐ d. was annoyed with Sid.

UP FROM SLAVERY
Booker T. Washington
13

The first place I went to in the North, was at Northampton, Massachusetts, where I spent nearly a half-day in looking for a colored family with whom I could board, never dreaming that any hotel would admit me. I was greatly surprised when I found that I would have no trouble in being accommodated at a hotel.

One might assume that the character of the passage was
☐ a. a radical student.
☐ b. too poor to pay for boarding in a hotel.
☐ c. a black person.
☐ d. not really satisfied with the thought of staying with "colored" persons.

THE ADVENTURES OF TOM SAWYER
Mark Twain
14

Now they stretched themselves out on their elbows and began to puff, charily, and with slender confidence. The smoke had an unpleasant taste, and they gagged a little, but Tom said:

"Why, it's just as easy! If I'd a knowed this was all, I'd a learnt long ago."

One may determine from this passage that
☐ a. the boys enjoyed smoking.
☐ b. Tom was putting up a good front.
☐ c. all boys try smoking.
☐ d. they would never smoke again.

19

SHOOTING AN ELEPHANT
George Orwell
15

... I marched down the hill, looking and feeling a fool, with the rifle over my shoulder and an ever-growing army of people jostling at my heels. At the bottom, when you got away from the huts, there was a metalled road and beyond that a miry waste of paddy fields a thousand yards across, not yet ploughed but soggy from the first rains and dotted with coarse grass. The elephant was standing eight yards from the road, his left side towards us.

He took not the slightest notice of the crowd's approach. He was tearing up bunches of grass, beating them against his knees to clean them and stuffing them into his mouth.

The passage leads one to surmise that
☐ a. the crowd is excited.
☐ b. the speaker is uncomfortable.
☐ c. the elephant will charge.
☐ d. the area is unsafe.

BAKER'S BLUEJAY YARN
Mark Twain
16

A jay hasn't got any more principle than a Congressman. A jay will lie, a jay will steal, a jay will deceive, a jay will betray; and four times out of five, a jay will go back on his solemnest promise. The sacredness of an obligation is a thing which you can't cram into no bluejay's head. Now, on top of all this, there's another thing; a jay can outswear any gentleman in the mines.... Yes sir, a jay is everything a man is!

From this description, we may infer that the author is
☐ a. bitter, to an extreme.
☐ b. critically humorous.
☐ c. informed about birds in general.
☐ d. an unhappy person.

TOM SAWYER ABROAD
Mark Twain
17

Well, by and by Tom's glory got to paling down gradu'ly, on account of other things turning up for the people to talk about—first, a horse-race, and on top of that a house afire, and on top of that the circus, and on top of that the eclipse; and that started a revival, same as it always does, and by that time there wasn't any more talk about Tom, so to speak, and you never see a person so sick and disgusted.

From Tom's feelings, as expressed in this paragraph, we can infer that he is somewhat
☐ a. shy.
☐ b. sociable.
☐ c. unselfish.
☐ d. self-centered.

ROBINSON CRUSOE
Daniel Defoe
18

He bid me observe it, and I should always find, that the calamities of life were shared among the upper and lower part of mankind; but that the middle station had the fewest disasters, and was not exposed to so many vicissitudes as the higher or lower part of mankind; nay, they were not subjected to so many distempers and uneasinesses either of body or mind as those were who, by vicious living, luxury, and extravagances on one hand or by hard labor, want of necessaries, and mean or insufficient diet on the other hand, bring distempers upon themselves by the natural consequences of their way of living; that the middle station of life was calculated for all kind of virtues and all kinds of enjoyment . . . .

It may be inferred as very likely, that the narrator
☐ a. hates money and what it buys.
☐ b. is repeating the words of a middle class person.
☐ c. dislikes the person whose words he's repeating.
☐ d. is usually disgruntled.

VICTORY
Joseph Conrad
19

Ricardo nodded, satisfied. Both these white men looked on native life as a mere play of shadows. A play of shadows the dominant race could walk through unaffected and disregarded in the pursuit of its incomprehensible aims and needs. No. Native craft did not count of course. It was an empty, solitary part of the sea, Schomberg expounded further.

These words imply a feeling of white
☐ a. compassion.
☐ b. understanding.
☐ c. superiority.
☐ d. appreciation.

THE MURDERS IN THE RUE MORGUE
Edgar Allan Poe
20

Oh, no; we had no conveniences for keeping him here. He is at a livery stable in the Rue Dubourg, just by. You can get him in the morning. Of course you are prepared to identify the property?

We may infer that the speaker is one who is
☐ a. unhappy about the situation.
☐ b. a thoughtless individual.
☐ c. not careful in his work.
☐ d. just doing his job.

OF HUMAN BONDAGE
Somerset Maugham
21

"If you had been a gentleman I think you'd have come next day and begged my pardon."

She had no mercy. He looked at her neck and thought how he would like to jab it with the knife he had for his muffin. He knew enough anatomy to make pretty certain of getting the carotid artery. And at the same time he wanted to cover her pale, thin face with kisses.

This passage leads one to judge that
☐ a. the speaker is kidding.
☐ b. the woman is teasing, playfully.
☐ c. the woman is the speaker's wife.
☐ d. the speaker has a serious conflict about his feelings for the woman.

THE MYSTERY OF EDWIN DROOD
Charles Dickens
22

Not only is the day waning, but the year. The low sun is fiery and yet cold behind the monastery ruin, and the Virginia creeper on the Cathedral wall has showered half its deep-red leaves down on the pavement. There has been rain this afternoon, and a wintry shudder goes among the little pools on the cracked uneven flagstones, and through the giant elm trees as they shed a gust of tears. Their fallen leaves lie strewn thickly about. Some of these leaves, in a timid rush, seek sanctuary within the low-arched Cathedral door, but two men coming out resist them, and cast them forth again with their feet; this done, one of the two locks the door with a goodly key and the other flits away with a folio musicbook.

One might presume, from this passage, that one of the men
☐ a. is angry with the other.
☐ b. is a musician.
☐ c. is a minister.
☐ d. is cold and hurries off.

MODERN INSTANCE
William D. Howells
23

The man who was munching cheese and crackers wore a hat rather large for him, pulled down over his eyes. He now said that he did not care if he took a gin-sling, and the bar-keeper promptly set it before him on the counter, and saluted with "Good evening, Colonel," a large man who came in, carrying a small dog in his arms. Bartley recognized him as the manager of a variety combination playing at one of the theatres, and the manager recognized the little man with the gin-sling as Tommy. He did not return the bar-keeper's salutation, but he asked, as he sat down at a table, "What do I want for supper, Charley?"

The Colonel gives us reason to believe that he wants Charley
☐ a. to be alert.
☐ b. to make selections for him.
☐ c. to pay attention to him.
☐ d. to mind his own business.

BLEAK HOUSE
Charles Dickens
24

"The old girl," says Mr. Bagnet in reply, "is a thoroughly fine woman. Consequently, she is like a thoroughly fine day. Gets finer as she gets on. I never saw the old girl's equal. But I never own to it before her. Discipline must be maintained!"

Mr. Bagnet's reply indicates that he
☐ a. isn't fair to his wife.
☐ b. doesn't appreciate his wife.
☐ c. is jealous of his wife's good qualities.
☐ d. is not entirely open with his wife.

A FAREWELL TO ARMS
Ernest Hemingway
25

I went to the window and looked out. The gravel paths were moist and the grass was wet with dew. The battery fired twice and the air came each time like a blow and shook the window and made the front of my pajamas flap. I could not see the guns but they were evidently firing directly over us. It was a nuisance to have them there but it was a comfort that they were no bigger. As I looked out at the garden I heard a motor truck starting on the road. I dressed, went downstairs, had some coffee in the kitchen and went out to the garage.

We may infer that the speaker views the situation
☐ a. with humor.
☐ b. as an outsider.
☐ c. with logic and calmness.
☐ d. with apprehension.

THE LOVED ONE
Evelyn Waugh
26

Later, at last, the time came when Aimee could decently depart; Mr. Joyboy saw her to the gate.

"I'd drive you home," he said, "only I don't like to leave Mom. The street car passes the corner. You'll be all right."

"Oh, I'll be all right," said Aimee.

"Mom just loved you."

"Did she?" said Aimee.

"Why yes. I always know. When Mom takes a fancy to people she treats them natural same as she treats me."

"She certainly treated me natural."

Mr. Joyboy quickly replied, "I'll say she did. Yes, she treated you natural and no mistake."

Mr. Joyboy appears to be
☐ a. very upset that Aimee must go by street car.
☐ b. more concerned with mother than Aimee.
☐ c. a strong, intelligent man.
☐ d. the perfect host.

THE OLD MAN AND THE SEA
Ernest Hemingway
27

The old man was thin and gaunt with deep wrinkles in the back of his neck. The brown blotches of the benevolent skin cancer the sun brings from its reflection on the tropic sea were on his cheeks. The blotches ran well down the sides of his face and his hands had the deep-creased scars from handling heavy fish on the cords. But none of these scars were fresh. They were as old as erosions in a fishless desert.

Judging from this passage, we could infer that the old man was
☐ a. dying.
☐ b. wealthy.
☐ c. a fisherman.
☐ d. friendly.

VICTORY
Joseph Conrad
28

He could not defend himself from compassion. He suggested that she might go to the consul, but it was his conscience that dictated this advice, not his conviction. She had never heard of the animal or of its uses. A consul! What was it? Who was he? What could he do? And when she learned that perhaps he could be induced to send her home, her head dropped on her breast.

One may conclude that the writer believes the consul to be
☐ a. very useful.
☐ b. of little use.
☐ c. known to very few people.
☐ d. a powerful figure.

TREASURE ISLAND
Robert Louis Stevenson
29

I remember him as if it were yesterday, as he came plodding to the inn door, his sea-chest following behind him in a hand-barrow; a tall, strong, heavy, nut-brown man; his tarry pig-tail falling over the shoulders of his soiled blue coat; his hands ragged and scarred, with black, broken nails, and the saber-cut across one cheek, a dirty, livid white. I remember him looking round the cove and whistling to himself as he did so, and then breaking out in that old seasong that he sung so often afterward:

"Fifteen men on the dead man's chest,
Yo-ho-ho and a bottle of rum!"

in the high, old tottering voice that seemed to have been tuned and broken at the capstan bars. Then he rapped on the door with a bit of stick like a handspike that he carried, and when my father appeared, called roughly for a glass of rum. This, when it was brought to him, he drank slowly, like a connoisseur, lingering on the taste, and still looking about him at the cliffs and up at our signboard.

From the description in this paragraph, the reader can infer that the captain
☐ a. was not accustomed to drinking.
☐ b. had never worked with his hands.
☐ c. had lived a hard, rough life.
☐ d. was a quiet, gentle man.

CANDIDE
Voltaire
30

Candide got well, and during his convalescence he had very good company to supper with him. They gambled for high stakes. Candide was quite amazed that he never got any aces, and Martin was not amazed at this at all.

This passage suggests that
☐ a. Candide's friends were very devoted.
☐ b. Candide was a poor card player.
☐ c. Martin was a man very rarely surprised.
☐ d. the honesty of Candide's companions was doubtful.

VICTORY
Joseph Conrad
31

"No, not so bad," Ricardo said, with indifference. "It's my opinion that men will gamble as long as they have anything to put on a card. Gamble? That's nature. What's life itself? You never know what may turn up. The worst of it is that you never can tell exactly what sort of cards you are holding yourself. What's trumps?—that is the question. See? Any man will gamble if only he's given a chance, for anything or everything. You too—"

Ricardo believes that gambling is
☐ a. impractical.
☐ b. evil.
☐ c. part of life.
☐ d. a good pastime.

THE ADVENTURES OF TOM SAWYER
Mark Twain
32

"I don't know, aunt."

"Well, I know. It's jam—that's what it is. Forty times I've said if you didn't let that jam alone I'd skin you. Hand me that switch."

The switch hovered in the air—the peril was desperate . . . .

"My! Look behind you, aunt!"

The old lady whirled round, and snatched her skirts out of danger. The lad fled, on the instant, scrambled up the highboard fence, and disappeared over it.

His aunt Polly stood surprised a moment, and then broke into a gentle laugh.

"Hang that boy, can't I ever learn anything?"

Aunt Polly's last comment leads us to believe that
☐ a. she was pleased that he ran away.
☐ b. this was a common occurrence.
☐ c. she never expected him to run.
☐ d. she didn't really want to punish him.

ABSALOM, ABSALOM
William Faulkner
33

"Now I want you to tell me just one thing more. Wh do you hate the South?"

"I don't hate it," Quenton said, quickly, at once, immediately;

"I don't hate it," he said. I don't hate it he thought; panting in the cold air, the iron New England dark; I don't. I don't! I don't hate it! I don't hate it!

Quentin's answer seems to indicate that
☐ a. the questioner was wrong.
☐ b. Quentin does hate the South.
☐ c. Quentin is from the North.
☐ d. the cold air affects Quentin.

BLEAK HOUSE
Charles Dickens
34

"This is my grandson," says Grandfather Smallweed. "You ha'n't seen him before. He is in the law, and not much at home."

"My service to him, too! He is like his sister. He is very like his sister. He is devilish like his sister," says Mr. George, laying a great and not altogether complimentary stress on his last adjective.

One may conclude from the passage that Mr. George
☐ a. is shocked at the appearance of the grandson.
☐ b. can't believe young Smallweed's resemblance to his sister.
☐ c. does not really see the resemblance.
☐ d. uses the word *devilish* to imply something about the grandson's character.

THE OLD MAN AND THE SEA
Ernest Hemingway
35

He is a great fish and I must convince him, he thought. I must never let him learn his strength nor what he could do if he made his run. If I were him I would put in everything now and go until something broke. But, thank God, they are not as intelligent as we who kill them; although they are more noble and more able....

It will uncramp though, he thought. Surely it will uncramp to help my right hand. There are three things that are brothers: the fish and my two hands. It must uncramp. It is unworthy of it to be cramped. The fish had slowed again and was going at his usual pace.

The old man's thoughts indicate that he and the fish are
☐ a. arch enemies.
☐ b. wise, strong, and noble.
☐ c. old and failing.
☐ d. doomed to kill one another.

THE GRAPES OF WRATH
John Steinbeck
36

And it came about that owners no longer worked on their farms. They farmed on paper; and they forgot the land, the smell, the feel of it, and remembered only that they owned it, remembered only what they gained and lost by it. And some of the farms grew so large that one man could not even conceive of them any more, so large that it took bookkeepers to keep track of interest and gain and loss; chemists to test the soil, to replenish; straw bosses to see that the stooping men were moving along the rows swiftly as the material of their bodies could stand.

The author most strongly implies that
☐ a. life on a farm is hard.
☐ b. farms have changed greatly.
☐ c. the changes on farms are for the worse.
☐ d. farms provide work for many people.

TYPEE
Herman Melville
37

These structures bear every indication of a very high antiquity, and Kory-Kory, who was my authority in all matters of scientific research, gave me to understand that they were coeval with the creation of the world; that the great gods themselves were the builders; and that they would endure until time shall be no more. Kory-Kory's prompt explanation, and his attributing the work to a divine origin, at once convinced me that neither he nor the rest of his countrymen knew anything about them.

One may assume from the passage that
☐ a. the speaker does not like Kory-Kory.
☐ b. the structures aren't valuable.
☐ c. the writer knows the actual age of the structures.
☐ d. the writer seriously doubts Kory-Kory's explanation.

THE TELL-TALE HEART
Edgar Allan Poe
38

It is impossible to say how first the idea entered my brain; but once conceived, it haunted me day and night. Object, there was none. Passion there was none. I loved the old man. He had never wronged me. He had never given me insult. For his gold I had no desire. I think it was his eye! Yes, it was this! He had the eye of a vulture—a pale blue eye, with a film over it. Whenever it fell upon me, my blood ran cold; and so by degrees—very gradually—I made up my mind to take the life of the old man, and thus rid myself of the eye forever.

One might conclude from the above passage that the speaker is
☐ a. patient.
☐ b. insane.
☐ c. an animal hater.
☐ d. without emotion.

A LAODICEAN
Thomas Hardy
39

Somerset looked at the youth, and said, "I fear I shall have to dispense with your services, Dare, for I think you have been tempted to-day."

"On my honour no. My manner is a little against me, Mr. Somerset. But you need not fear for my ability to do your work. I am a young man wasted, and am thought of slight account: it is the true men who get snubbed, while traitors are allowed to thrive!"

It appears from this passage that
☐ a. Dare is humble.
☐ b. Somerset wishes to fire Dare.
☐ c. the young man can't do the work.
☐ d. Somerset is unreasonable.

TYPEE
Herman Melville
40

In looking back to this period, and calling to remembrance the numberless proofs of kindness and respect which I received from the natives of the valley, I can scarcely understand it was that, in the midst of so many consolatory circumstances, my mind should still have been consumed by the most dismal forebodings, and have remained a prey to the profoundest melancholy. It is true that the suspicious circumstances which had attended the disappearance of Toby were enough of themselves to excite distrust with regard to the savages, in whose power I felt myself to be entirely placed, especially when it was combined with the knowledge that these very men, kind and respectful as they were to me, were, after all, nothing better than a set of cannibals.

The reader may surmise that the speaker's feelings toward the natives are
☐ a. conflicting.
☐ b. hostile.
☐ c. loving.
☐ d. condescending.

VICTORY
Joseph Conrad
41

He felt himself more in danger, nearer death, than ever since he had entered that room. An insane bandit is a deadly combination. He did not, could not know that Mr. Jones was quick-minded enough to see already the end of his reign over his excellent secretary's thoughts and feelings; the coming failure of Ricardo's fidelity. A woman had intervened! A woman, a girl, who apparently possessed the power to awaken men's disgusting folly. Her power had been proved in two instances already—the beastly innkeeper, and that man with moustaches, upon whom Mr. Jones, his deadly right hand twitching in his pocket, glared more in repulsion than in anger.

The feeling in this passage leads one to conclude that
☐ a. the woman is a part of the criminal's plan.
☐ b. it's all a misunderstanding.
☐ c. danger has been mounting gradually.
☐ d. Mr. Jones is calm.

THE MARRIAGES
Henry James
42

I was not rich—on the contrary; and I had been told the Pension Beaurepas was cheap. I had moreover been told that a boardinghouse is a capital place for the study of human nature. I had a fancy for a literary career, and a friend of mine had said to me, "If you mean to write, you ought to go and live in a boardinghouse; there is no other such place to pick up material." I had read something of this kind in a letter addressed by Stendhal to his sister: "I have a passionate desire to know human nature, and have a great mind to live in a boardinghouse, where people cannot conceal their real characters."

The speaker implies to the reader that he
☐ a. can't make up his own mind.
☐ b. is stingy with money.
☐ c. is really serious about writing.
☐ d. likes to move from one boarding house to the other.

CANDIDE
Voltaire
43

Cacambo manifested all his curiosity to his host; the host said to him: "I am very ignorant, and I get along all right that way; but we have here an old man who has retired from the court, who is the most learned man in the kingdom and the most communicative." Immediately he took Cacambo to the old man. Candide was now playing only second fiddle and going along with his valet. They entered a house that was very simple, for the door was only of silver and the paneling in the apartments only of gold, but wrought with so much taste that the richest paneling did not eclipse it. True, the antechamber was encrusted only with rubies and emeralds, but the order in which everything was arranged fully made up for this extreme simplicity.

One may infer from the passage that
☐ a. Cacambo is in a land in which everyone is friendly.
☐ b. the kingdom in which the old man lives is very rich.
☐ c. the old man is the king.
☐ d. everyone in the kingdom leads a very simple life.

PULL DOWN VANITY
Leslie A. Fiedler
44

I worked then only on Saturdays, thinking of those twelve hours in a shoestore as a parenthesis in my life. I remember myself on the way to work, the only one it seemed to me then fully awake among the half-sleeping adult workers on the streetcar. I can still feel my eagerness and my fear; and for the moment I seem to be jolted again on the straw seat, my hair damp and unnaturally plastered back. I am wearing knickers; I have never shaved.

The speaker implies that in this part of his youth
☐ a. he was generally optimistic.
☐ b. he hated his routine.
☐ c. he disliked adults.
☐ d. he wanted to become a shoe salesman, permanently.

BARCHESTER TOWERS
Anthony Trollope
45

This narrative is supposed to commence immediately after the installation of Dr. Proudie. I will not describe the ceremony, as I do not precisely understand its nature. I am ignorant whether a bishop be chaired like a member of Parliament, or carried in a gilt coach like a lord mayor, or sworn in like a justice of peace, or introduced like a peer to the upper house, or led between two brethren like a knight of the garter; but I do know that everything was properly done and that nothing fit or becoming to a young bishop was omitted on the occasion.

The author indicates that the speaker must have known by instinct
☐ a. that he could never figure out the ceremony.
☐ b. that he was incapable of doing his task well.
☐ c. that the ceremony went well.
☐ d. that one is serious on such occasions.

BLEAK HOUSE
Charles Dickens
46

The fair Volumnia being one of those sprightly girls who cannot long continue silent without imminent peril of seizure by the dragon Boredom, soon indicates the approach of that monster with a series of undisguisable yawns. Finding it impossible to suppress those yawns by any other process than conversation, she compliments Mrs. Rouncewell on her son; declaring that he positively is one of the finest figures she ever saw, and as soldierly a looking person she should think, as what's his name, her favourite Life Guardsman—the man she dotes on—the darest of creatures—who was killed at Waterloo.

From the description in this passage, Volumnia seems
☐ a. thoughtful.
☐ b. self centered.
☐ c. serious.
☐ d. understanding.

35

TREASURE ISLAND
Robert Louis Stevenson
47

... the two lads fell in love, and that with the same lady. Mr. Ebenezer, who was the admired and the beloved, and the spoiled one, made, no doubt, mighty certain of the victory; and when he found he had deceived himself, screamed like a peacock. The whole country heard of it; now he lay sick at home, with his silly family standing round the bed in tears; now he rode from public-house to public-house and shouted his sorrows into the lug of Tom, Dick, and Harry. Your father, Mr. David, was a kind gentleman; but he was weak, dolefully weak; took all this folly with a long countenance; and one day—by your leave!—resigned the lady. She was no such fool, however; it's from her you must inherit your excellent good sense; and she refused to be bandied from one to another. Both got upon their knees to her; and the upshot of the matter for that while, was that she showed both of them the door.

This passage is rich with implications that
☐ a. the lady was a poor choice.
☐ b. the lady was more poised than both men.
☐ c. Mr. Ebenezer really didn't love her.
☐ d. Mr. David didn't deserve her.

THE ADVENTURES OF RODERICK RANDOM
Tabias Smollett
48

In the meantime, the storm subsided into a brisk gale, that carried us into the warm latitudes, where the weather became intolerable, and the crew very sickly. The doctor left nothing unattempted towards the completion of his vengeance against the Welshman and me. He went among the sick, under pretense of inquiring into their grievances, with a view of picking up complaints to our prejudice.

The speaker indicates that
☐ a. the crew had a deadly disease.
☐ b. the doctor was sick, too.
☐ c. the doctor had a vengeful nature.
☐ d. the speaker wasn't ill.

MEN'S WIVES
William M. Thackeray
49

Well, Mrs. Crump's little grandchild was born, entirely to the dissatisfaction, I must say, of his father; who, when the infant was brought to him in the Fleet, had him abruptly covered up in his cloak again, from which he had been removed by the jealous prison door-keepers; why, do you think? Walter had a quarrel with one of them, and the wretch persisted in believing that the bundle Mrs. Crump was bringing to her son-in-law was a bundle of disguised brandy!

We can assume from this passage that
☐ a. the small infant was premature.
☐ b. the father disliked Mrs. Crump.
☐ c. the brandy bottles, at that time, were large.
☐ d. there was hostility between the father and mother.

SISTER CARRIE
Theodore Dreiser
50

Carrie was certainly better than this man, as she was superior, mentally, to Drouet. She came fresh from the air of the village, the light of the country still in her eye. Here was neither guile nor rapacity. There was slight inherited traits of both in her, but they were rudimentary. She was too full of wonder and desire to be greedy. She still looked about her upon the great maze of the city without understanding. Hurstwood felt the bloom and the youth. He picked her as he would the fresh fruit of a tree. He felt as fresh in her presence as one who is taken out of the flash of summer to the first cool breath of spring.

One is led to believe that Carrie's most desirable trait is
☐ a. intelligence.
☐ b. innocence.
☐ c. ambition.
☐ d. beauty.

EVERYTHING THAT RISES MUST CONVERGE
Flannery O'Connor
51

Mrs. May's bedroom window was low and faced on the east and the bull, silvered in the moonlight, stood under it, his head raised as if he listened—like some patient god come down to woo her—for a stir inside the room. The window was dark and the sound of her breathing too light to be carried outside. Clouds crossing the moon blackened him and in the dark he began to tear at the hedge. Presently they passed and he appeared again in the same spot, chewing steadily, with a hedge-wreath that he had ripped loose for himself caught in the tips of his horns. When the moon drifted into retirement again, there was nothing to mark his place but the sound of steady chewing. Then abruptly a pink glow filled the window. Bars of light slid across him as the venetian blind was slit. He took a step backward and lowered his head as if to show the wreath across his horns.

One may infer from the passage that
☐ a. Mrs. May lived on a farm.
☐ b. the animal was astray.
☐ c. there was danger from the bull.
☐ d. the garden was being ruined.

GREENLEAF
Flannery O'Connor
52

She sat in the car and watched him stalk off toward the harness room where he kept a gun. After he had entered the room, there was a crash as if he had kicked something out of his way. Presently he emerged again with the gun, circled behind the car, opened the door violently, and threw himself onto the seat beside her. He held the gun between his knees and looked straight ahead. He'd like to shoot me instead of the bull, she thought, and turned her face away so that he could not see her smile.

The woman described here is feeling
☐ a. jeopardized.   ☐ c. distracted.
☐ b. triumphant.   ☐ d. powerless.

GULLIVER'S TRAVELS
Jonathan Swift
53

When I found myself on my feet, I looked about me, and must confess I never beheld a more entertaining prospect. The country round appeared like a continued garden, and the enclosed fields, which were generally forty foot square, resembled so many beds of flowers. These fields were intermingled with woods of half a stang, and the tallest trees, as I could judge, appeared to be seven foot high. I viewed the town on my left hand, which looked like a painted scene of a city in a theatre.

The speaker leads one to believe that
☐ a. he's in a theater.
☐ b. he's lost and concerned about it.
☐ c. he's frightened by what he sees.
☐ d. he's intrigued by this place.

JANE EYRE
Charlotte Brontë
54

While arranging my hair, I looked at my face in the glass, and felt it was no longer plain: there was hope in its aspect, and life in its colour: and my eyes seemed as if they had beheld the fount of fruition, and borrowed beams from the lustrous ripple. I had often been unwilling to look at my master, because I feared he could not be pleased at my looks; but I was sure I might lift my face to his now, and not cool his affection by its expression. I took a plain but clean and light summer dress from my drawer and put it on: it seemed no attire had ever so well become me; because none had I ever worn in so blissful a mood.

The speaker's words lead one to surmise that
☐ a. she is vain.
☐ b. she cannot face the truth about herself.
☐ c. she feels happiness makes one look pretty.
☐ d. she hates her master.

MAIN TRAVELLED ROADS
Hamlin Garland
55

The girl put her elbows on the fence, and watched her little brother as he sped away to the pool, throwing off his clothes as he ran, whooping with uncontrollable delight. Soon she could hear him splashing about in the water a short distance up the stream, and caught glimpses of his little shiny body and happy face. How cool that water looked! And the shadows there by the big basswood! How that water would cool her blistered feet! An impulse seized her, and she squeezed between the rails of the fence, and stood in the road looking up and down to see that the way was clear. It was not a main-travelled road; no one was likely to come; why not?

From the content of the passage it seems that the girl wishes to
☐ a. sit by the water.
☐ b. invite others to swim.
☐ c. wade in the water.
☐ d. take off her clothes and swim, too.

THE RED BADGE OF COURAGE
Stephen Crane
56

All about them were other small fires surrounded by men with their little black utensils. From one of these near came sudden sharp voices in a row. It appeared that two light-footed soldiers had been teasing a huge, bearded man, causing him to spill coffee upon his blue knees. The man had gone into a rage and had sworn comprehensively. Stung by his language, his tormentors had immediately bristled at him with a great show of resenting unjust oaths. Possibly there was going to be a fight.

The implication, here, is that
☐ a. the bearded man is pretending.
☐ b. the soldiers are just fun loving.
☐ c. everyone is sleepy.
☐ d. tempers are short.

VICTORY
Joseph Conrad
57

The loose silver, some guilders and dollars, I have always kept in that unlocked left drawer. I have no doubt Wang knows what there is in it; but he isn't a thief, and that's why I—no, Lena, what I've missed is not gold or jewels; and that's what makes the fact interesting—which the theft of money cannot be.

One may infer from the passage that the speaker
☐ a. thinks that theft is natural.
☐ b. is not sure of his possessions.
☐ c. cares very little about money.
☐ d. has more money than he actually needs.

THE SUN ALSO RISES
Ernest Hemingway
58

He was Spider Kelly's star pupil. Spider Kelly taught all his young gentlemen to box like featherweights, no matter whether they weighed one hundred and five or two hundred and five pounds. But it seemed to fit Cohn. He was really very fast. He was so good that Spider promptly overmatched him and got his nose permanently flattened. This increased Cohn's distaste for boxing, but it gave him a certain satisfaction of some strange sort, and it certainly improved his nose. In his last year at Princeton he read too much and took to wearing spectacles. I never met any one of his class who remembered him. They did not even remember that he was middleweight boxing champion.

From reading the above passage, one might infer that the character of Cohn is
☐ a. unimpressive.
☐ b. overbearing.
☐ c. strange.
☐ d. attractive.

LOST HORIZON
James Hilton
59

The plane was swooping down at a tremendous speed, and as it did so, the air grew hotter; the scorched earth below was like an oven with the door suddenly opened. One mountain top after another lifted itself above the horizon in craggy silhouette; now the flight was along a curving valley, the base of which was strewn with rocks and debris of dried-up watercourses. It looked like a floor littered with nut-shells. The plane bumped and tossed in air-pockets as uncomfortably as a rowboat in a swell. All four passengers had to hold on to their seats.

"Looks like he wants to land!" shouted the American hoarsely.

"He can't!" Mallinson retorted. "He'd simply be mad if he tried to! He'll crash and then—"

The indications are that the persons speaking are
☐ a. the passengers.
☐ b. observers on the ground.
☐ c. observers from the tower.
☐ d. a passenger and stewardess.

THE MARRIAGES
Henry James
60

Godfrey was in working gear—shirt and trousers and slippers and a beautiful silk jacket. His room felt hot, though a window was open to the summer night; the lamp on the table shed its studious light over a formidable heap of textbooks and papers, and the bed showed that he had flung himself down to think out a problem. As soon as she got in she said to him: "Father's going to marry Mrs. Churchley!"

One may assume that Godfrey was
☐ a. an introvert.
☐ b. probably hard to get along with.
☐ c. a studious person.
☐ d. annoyed with himself.

A MODERN INSTANCE
William D. Howell
61

The Halleck girls went early in July to the Profile House, where they had spent their summers for many years; but the old people preferred to stay at home, and only left their large, comfortable house for short absences. Their ways of life had been fixed in other times, and Mrs. Halleck liked better than mountain or sea, the high-walled garden that stretched back to their house to the next street. They had bought through to this street when they built, but they had never sold the lot that fronted on it.

One can best assume
- ☐ a. that the "old people" are the girls' parents.
- ☐ b. the Profile home is owned by the Hallecks.
- ☐ c. the girls preferred the Profile House to their own home all the time.
- ☐ d. the garden was well cultivated.

BLEAK HOUSE
Charles Dickens
62

An ugly woman, very poorly clothed, hurried in while I was glancing at them, and coming straight up to the mother, said, "Jenny! Jenny!" All the rest was in the tone in which she said them.

She also had upon her face and arms the marks of ill-usage. She had no kind of grace about her, but the grace of sympathy; but when she condoled with the woman, and her own tears fell, she wanted no beauty. I say condoled, but her only words were "Jenny! Jenny!" All the rest was in the tone in which she said them.

The speaker concludes that he learned most about the ugly woman
- ☐ a. from the words she spoke.
- ☐ b. from the manner in which she spoke them.
- ☐ c. from her tears.
- ☐ d. from her poor clothing.

OUR HEARTS WERE YOUNG AND GAY
Cornelia Otis Skinner and Emily Kimbrough
63

Finally into Emily's desperate eye there came a glint of determination. With the pent-up frenzy of despair she aimed and instead of twirling the ring, threw it like a baseball. This time there was no boomerang action. Swift as an arrow that rope doughnut shot at a tangent from the court, over the heads of the rapturous audience, down to the second-class promenade and spun the cap off an officer who was just coming out on deck. Cap and missle went overboard and the officer turned right around and went back inside. That formed a sort of climax. The match was declared null or void or something and the three men shook hands but I don't remember anyone shaking hands with Emily.

One might conclude that Emily
☐ a. knew how to play the game.
☐ b. would be asked to play again.
☐ c. should avoid her partners for awhile.
☐ d. should have won.

MOLL FLANDERS
Daniel Defoe
64

This woman had also a little school, which she kept to teach children to read and to work; and having, I say, lived before that in good fashion, she bred up the children she took with a great deal of art, as well as with a great deal of care.

The inference, based on this passage, is that
☐ a. the woman was an artist.
☐ b. the woman had no family of her own.
☐ c. the woman had wealth.
☐ d. the woman took great pride in her work.

TO KILL A MOCKINGBIRD
Harper Lee
65

The remainder of my schooldays were no more auspicious than the first. Indeed, they were an endless Project that slowly evolved into a Unit, in which miles of construction paper and wax crayon were expended by the State of Alabama in its well-meaning but fruitless efforts to teach me Group Dynamics.

The speaker implies that
☐ a. the first part of his education was fruitful.
☐ b. he thinks little of the value of his education.
☐ c. he prefers scholarly endeavors to projects.
☐ d. he holds Alabama responsible for his failure.

SISTER CARRIE
Theodore Dreiser
66

Each day he could read in the evening papers of the doings within this walled city. In the notices of passengers for Europe he read the names of eminent frequenters of his old resort. In the theatrical column appeared, from time to time, announcements of the latest successes of men he had known. He knew that they were at their old gayeties. Pullmans were hauling them to and fro about the land, papers were greeting them with interesting mentions, the elegant lobbies of hotels and the glow of polished dining-rooms were keeping them close within the walled city. Men whom he had known, men whom he had tipped glasses with—rich men, and he was forgotten! Who was Mr. Wheeler? What was the Warren Street resort? Bah!

The writer implies that Hurstwood places great value on
☐ a. adventure.
☐ b. travel.
☐ c. prestige.
☐ d. friendship.

KON-TIKI
Thor Heyerdahl
67

But the explanation of the whole mystery was lacking. Who were these people, and where had they come from?

One can safely say that the answers to these riddles have been nearly as many in number as the works which have treated them. Specialists in different fields have put forth quite different solutions, but their affirmations have always been disproved later by logical arguments from experts who have worked along other lines. Malaya, India, China, Japan, Arabia, Egypt, the Caucasus, Atlantis, even Germany and Norway, have been seriously championed as the Polynesians' homeland. But every time some obstacle of a decisive character has appeared and put the whole problem into the melting pot again.

It is reasonable to conclude that
☐ a. knowledge about these people isn't really important.
☐ b. experts are very eager to solve this problem.
☐ c. it's impossible to solve the problem.
☐ d. the so-called experts aren't very capable.

A LAODICEAN
Thomas Hardy
68

"It was ill-considered of me, however" he said; "and in his distress he has forgotten his Bible." He went and picked up the worn volume from where it lay on the grass.

"You can easily win him to forgive you, by just following, and returning the book to him," she observed.

"I will," said the young man impulsively. And bowing to her, he hastened along the river brink after the minister.

One can assume, after reading the above passage that the
☐ a. man and woman had a slight disagreement.
☐ b. female hated to observe the dispute.
☐ c. the minister and man had some sort of disagreement.
☐ d. the woman and man had hurt the minister's feelings.

BLEAK HOUSE
Charles Dickens
69

Now, does Sir Leicester become worse; restless, uneasy, and in great pain. Volumnia lighting a candle (with a pre-destined aptitude for doing something objectionable) is bidden to put it out again, for it is not yet dark enough. Yet it is very dark too; as dark as it will be all night. By-and-by she tries again. No! Put it out. It is not dark enough yet.

One may infer from the passage that
☐ a. Volumnia is purposely trying to annoy Sir Leicester.
☐ b. Sir Leicester is afraid to admit that it is getting late.
☐ c. Sir Leicester wants Volumnia to leave the room.
☐ d. Volumnia is afraid of the dark.

VANITY FAIR
William M. Thackeray
70

We must pass over a part of Mrs. Rebecca Crawley's biography with that lightness and delicacy which the world demands—the moral world that has, perhaps, no particular objection to vice, but an insuperable repugnance to hearing vice called by its proper name. There are things we do and know perfectly well in Vanity Fair, though we never speak of them.

The author intimates that people of Vanity Fair are
☐ a. sinful.
☐ b. moral.
☐ c. repugnant.
☐ d. hypocritical.

IN BLACK AND WHITE
Rudyard Kipling
71

Love knows no caste; else why should I, a Musalman and the son of a Musalman, have sought a Hindu woman—a widow of the Hindus—the sister of the headman of Pateera? But it was even so. They of the headman's household came on a pilgrimage to Muttra when She was but newly a bride. Silver tires were upon the wheels of the bullock-cart, and silken curtains hid the woman. Sahib, I made no haste in their conveyance, for the wind parted the curtains and I saw Her.

One might assume that the Musalmen
☐ a. was impractical and foolish.
☐ b. was sufficiently infatuated to pursue the woman.
☐ c. cared what others thought.
☐ d. could never win this woman.

MEN'S WIVES
William M. Thackeray
72

But Woolsey humbly said he was not a riding man, and gladly consented to take a place in the Clarence carriage, provided he was allowed to bear half the expenses of the entertainment. This proposal was agreed to by Mr. Eglantine, and the two gentlemen parted to meet once more at the "Kidneys" that night, when everybody was edified by the friendly tone adopted between them.

One might assume
☐ a. there would be some live entertainment in the carriage.
☐ b. that Mr. Eglantine was a riding man.
☐ c. Woolsey probably could ride but at the moment didn't choose to.
☐ d. that Woolsey was reasonable and affable.

SISTER CARRIE
Theodore Dreiser
73

Hurstwood was an interesting character after his kind. He was shrewd and clever in many little things, and capable of creating a good impression. His managerial position was fairly important—a kind of stewardship which was imposing, but lacked financial control. He had risen by perseverance and industry, through long years of service, from the position of barkeeper in a commonplace, set off in polished cherry and grill-work, where he kept, in a roll-top desk, the rather simple accounts of the place—supplies ordered and needed. The chief executive and financial functions devolved upon the owners—Messrs. Fitzgerald and Moy—and upon a cashier who looked after the money taken in.

The writer suggests that
- ☐ a. Hurstwood's job needs a more capable person.
- ☐ b. Hurstwood is in a position of high authority.
- ☐ c. Hurstwood's position seems much more impressive than it really is.
- ☐ d. Hurstwood's employers depend upon him to run their business.

VICTORY
Joseph Conrad
74

Ricardo shook his head in silence and looked expectant. With him Schomberg exchanged at least twenty words every day. He was infinitely more communicative than his patron. At times he looked very much like an ordinary human being of his class; and he seemed to be in an amiable mood at that moment. Suddenly spreading some ten cards face downward in the form of a fan, he thrust them towards Schomberg.

One may infer that Ricardo's patron is
- ☐ a. in control of Ricardo's behavior.
- ☐ b. unaware of his meeting with Schomberg.
- ☐ c. very communicative.
- ☐ d. not at all communicative.

BLEAK HOUSE
Charles Dickens
75

I said it certainly was not business that I came upon, but it was not quite a pleasant matter.

"Then, my dear Miss Summerson," said he [Mr. Skimpole], with the frankest gaiety, "don't allude to it. Why should you allude to anything that is not a pleasant matter? I never do. And you are a much pleasanter creature, in every point of view, than I. You are perfectly pleasant; I am imperfectly pleasant; then, if I never allude to an unpleasant matter, how much less should you! So, that's disposed of, and we will talk of something else."

Mr. Skimpole's argument indicates that he
☐ a. is quick to recognize his own feelings.
☐ b. is mainly concerned about Miss Summerson's feelings.
☐ c. is aware of only the pleasant things in life.
☐ d. wants to ignore anything unpleasant in life.

BLEAK HOUSE
Charles Dickens
76

"But Guardian, may we not hope that a little experience will teach him what a false and wretched thing it is?"

"We will hope so, my Esther," said Mr. Jarndyce, "and that it may not teach him so too late. In any case we must not be hard on him. There are not many grown and matured men living while we speak, good men, too, who, if they were thrown into this same court as suitors, would not be vitally changed and depreciated within three years—within two—within one. How can we stand amazed at poor Rick?"

We may conclude that Mr. Jarndyce
☐ a. has almost no hope for Rick.
☐ b. is sure of a change in Rick's attitude.
☐ c. is more optimistic than Esther.
☐ d. does not want to build up Esther's hopes too much.

THE RISE OF SILAS LAPHAM
William D. Howells
77

There was a light crash, and the mare recoiled her length, and separated their wheels from those of the open buggy in front which Lapham had driven into. He made his excuses to the occupant; and the accident relieved the tension of their feelings, and left them far from the point of mutual injury which they had reached in their common trouble and their unselfish will for their children's good.

The passage gives reason to believe that
☐ a. one buggy was badly damaged.
☐ b. the mare had rolled up on the ground.
☐ c. the occupants had been angry before the crash.
☐ d. someone was careless.

A CASE OF IDENTITY
Arthur Conan Doyle
78

"Do you not find," he said, "that with your short sight it is a little trying to do so much typewriting?"

"I did at first," she answered, "but now I know where the letters are without looking." Then, suddenly realizing the full purport of his words she gave a violent start and looked up, with fear and astonishment upon her broad, good-humoured face. "You've heard about me, Mr. Holmes," she cried, "else how could you know all that?"

"Never mind," said Holmes, laughing; "it is my business to know things. Perhaps I have trained myself to see what others overlook. If not, why should you come to consult me?"

One may reasonably assume that Mr. Holmes
☐ a. deals in investigations.
☐ b. is prying without need.
☐ c. knows the woman well.
☐ d. is just guessing.

SISTER CARRIE
Theodore Dreiser
79

As a matter of fact, she was in a most hopeless quandary. Here was a man [Hurstwood] whom she thoroughly liked, who exercised an influence over her, sufficient almost to delude her into the belief that she was possessed of a lively passion for him. She was still the victim of his keen eyes, his suave manners, his fine clothes. She looked and saw before her a man who was most gracious and sympathetic, who leaned toward her with a feeling that was a delight to observe. She could hardly keep from feeling what he felt.

One may infer from the passage that Carrie
☐ a. pities Hurstwood because she has no feeling for him.
☐ b. is afraid to tell Hurstwood of her love for him.
☐ c. would like to care more for Hurstwood than she actually does.
☐ d. wants Hurstwood only because of his wealth.

VICTORY
Joseph Conrad
80

"He has me at his mercy now," thought Heyst, without particular excitement.

The sentiment he experienced was curiosity. He forgot himself in it; it was as if he were considering somebody else's strange predicament. But even that sort of interest was dying out when, looking to his left, he saw the accustomed shapes of the other bungalows looming in the night, and remembered the arrival of the thirsty company in the boat. Wang would hardly risk such a crime in the presence of other white men. It was a peculiar instance of the "safety in numbers" principle, which somehow was not much to Heyst's taste.

It is clear from the passage that Heyst
☐ a. is worried about his safety.
☐ b. knows Wang better than the other men.
☐ c. cares nothing about other people.
☐ d. cares little about preserving his life.

THE DYNASTS
Thomas Hardy
81

First Old Man: How d'ye make that out, when th'st never been to school?

Second Old Man: I larned it at church, thank God.

First Old Man: Church? What have God A'mighty got to do with profane knowledge? Beware what you be saying, Jems Purchess!

Second Old Man: I say I did, whether or no. Twas the zingers up in gallery that I had it from. They busted out that strong with "the round world and they that dwell therein," that we common fokes down under could no less than believe 'em.

A careful reading of the passage implies that the first old man's question concerned
☐ a. a chance to sing in the gallery.
☐ b. the roundness of the world.
☐ c. the second old man's truthfulness.
☐ d. a way to pray.

THE OLD MAN AND THE SEA
Ernest Hemingway
82

"It was the only way to kill him," the old man said.... He's over fifteen hundred pounds the way he is, he thought. Maybe much more. If he dresses out two-thirds of that at thirty cents a pound?"

"I need a pencil for that," he said. "My head is not that clear. But I think the great Joe DiMaggio would be proud of me today. I had no bone spurs. But the hands and the back hurt truly." I wonder what a bone spur is, he thought. Maybe we have them without knowing of it.

Hemingway implies that humans
☐ a. can overcome their limitations and fears.
☐ b. are weakened by physical misfortunes.
☐ c. are the masters of other animals and fishes.
☐ d. need national heroes to drive them on.

TYPEE
Herman Melville
83

Let the savages be civilized, but civilize them with benefits, and not with evils; and let heathenism be destroyed, but not by destroying the heathen. The Anglo-Saxon hive have extirpated Paganism from the greater part of the North American continent; but with it they have likewise extirpated the greater portion of the Red race. Civilization is gradually sweeping from the earth the lingering vestiges of Paganism, and at the same time the shrinking forms of its unhappy worshippers.

The author seems to indicate that
☐ a. Indians are not worth saving.
☐ b. the end does not justify the means.
☐ c. heathenism and Christianity are equally important.
☐ d. Anglo-Saxons are always right.

THE MYSTERY OF EDWIN DROOD
Charles Dickens
84

Shaking from head to foot, the man whose scattered consciousness has thus fantastically pieced itself together at length rises, supports his trembling frame upon his arms, and looks around. He is in the meanest and closest of small rooms. Through the ragged window-curtain the light of early day steals in from a miserable court. He lies dressed, across a large unseemly bed, upon a bedstead that has indeed given way under the weight upon it. Lying, also dressed and also across the bed, not longwise, are a Chinaman, a Lascar, and a haggard woman. The two first are in a sleep or stupor; the last is blowing at a kind of pipe, to kindle it.

The information which this passage gives indicates that
☐ a. the first man is waking from a normal night's rest.
☐ b. the first man is drunk.
☐ c. something drastic has taken place.
☐ d. the people are friends.

BLEAK HOUSE
Charles Dickens
85

"At least there is no opposition to you," Volumnia asserts with confidence.

"No, Volumnia. This distracted country has lost its senses in many respects, I grieve to say, but—"

Volumnia's finishing the sentence restores her to favour. Sir Leicester, with a gracious inclination of his head, seems to say to himself, "A sensible woman this, on the whole, though occasionally precipitate."

Sir Leicester's favour for Volumnia seems to depend upon her
☐ a. agreeing with him.
☐ b. good sense.
☐ c. careful observation.
☐ d. being a good listener.

VICTORY
Joseph Conrad
86

Suddenly, remembering the occasion of that "fracas," Schomberg groaned with the pain as of a hot coal under his breastbone, and gave himself up to desolation. Ah, if he only had that girl with him he would have been masterful and resolute and fearless—fight twenty desperadoes—care for nobody on earth! Whereas the possession of Mrs. Schomberg was no incitement of a display of manly virtues. Instead of caring for no one, he felt that he cared for nothing. Life was a hollow sham; he wasn't going to risk a shot through his lungs or his liver in order to preserve its integrity. It had no savour—damn it!

One may assume, from this passage, that
☐ a. life is meaningless for Schomberg.
☐ b. he is unhappy with his wife in all circumstances.
☐ c. he fears he lacks manly virtues.
☐ d. his life in in grave danger.

ANNA KARENINA
Leo Tolstoy
87

"Oh, it's awful! oh dear! oh dear! awful!" Stepan Arkadyevitch kept repeating to himself, and he could think of nothing to be done. "And how well things were going up till now! how well we got on! She was contented and happy in her children; I never interfered with her in anything; I let her manage the children and the house just as she liked. It's true it's bad *her* having been a governess in our home. That's bad! There's something common, vulgar, in flirting with one's governess. But what a governess!" (He vividly recalled the roguish black eyes of Mlle. Roland and her smile.) "But after all, while she was in the house, I kept myself in hand. And the worst of it all is that she's already . . . it seems as if ill-luck would have it so! Oh, oh! But what, what is to be done?"

Stepan Arkadyevitch's thoughts suggest that he
☐ a. was despondent over his own vulgarity.
☐ b. only partially regretted his affair.
☐ c. had a very close relationship with his wife.
☐ d. had completely repented for his behavior.

MEN'S WIVES
William M. Thackeray
88

What this jovial party ate for dinner at the "Star and Garter" need not here be set down. If they did not drink champagne I am very much mistaken. They were as merry as any four people in Christendom; and between the bewildering attentions of the perfumer, and the manly courtesy of the tailor, Morgiana very likely forgot the gallant Captain, or, at least, was very happy in his absence.

The author implies that Morgiana
☐ a. was very loyal to the Captain.
☐ b. took good advantage of every opportunity.
☐ c. became tense at dinner parties.
☐ d. didn't really know anyone.

BLEAK HOUSE
Charles Dickens
89

"For I am constantly being taken in these nets," said Mr. Skimpole, looking beamingly at us over a glass of wine-and-water, "and am constantly being bailed out—like a boat. Or paid off—like a ship's company. Somebody always does it for me. I can't do it, you know, for I never have any money. But Somebody does it. I get out by Somebody's means; I am not like the starling; I get out. If you were to ask me who Somebody is, upon my word I couldn't tell you. Let us drink to Somebody. God bless him!"

From the passage, one may infer that Mr. Skimpole
☐ a. is ashamed of his helplessness.
☐ b. enjoys his lack of responsibility.
☐ c. is incapable of managing his financial affairs.
☐ d. is anxious about his financial state.

ANTIGONE
Sophocles
90

You cannot learn of any man the soul,
the mind, and the intent until he shows
his practise of the government and law.
For I believe that who controls the state
and does not hold to the best plans of all,
but locks his tongue up through some kind of fear,
that he is worst of all who are or were.
And he who counts another greater friend
than his own fatherland, I put him nowhere.

The speaker is most likely to admire a man who
☐ a. is a dictator.
☐ b. puts friendship above all else.
☐ c. wishes the best for his country and people.
☐ d. gives in easily.

57

BLEAK HOUSE
Charles Dickens
91

I don't know how it is, I seem to be always writing about myself. I mean all the time to write about other people, and I try to think about myself as little as possible, and I am sure, when I find myself coming into the story again, I am really vexed and say, "Dear, dear, you tiresome little creature, I wish you wouldn't!" but it is all of no use. I hope any one who may read what I write, will understand that if these pages contain a great deal about me, I can only suppose it must be because I have really something to do with them, and can't be kept out.

One may infer from the passage that the speaker
- a. is self-centered.
- b. knows very little about the world.
- c. feels self-conscious.
- d. has very little self-control.

ANTIGONE
Sophocles
92

Wandering hope brings help to many men.
But others she tricks from their godly loves,
and her quarry knows nothing until he has walked into flame.
Word of wisdom it was when someone said,
"The bad becomes the good
to him a god would doom."
Only briefly is that one from under doom.

The speaker seems to feel that
- a. hope can be helpful, but is often misleading.
- b. men are fools to be lead on by hope when they are doomed.
- c. he that confuses good and bad is doomed.
- d. one never knows when one is doomed until it's too late.

WAR AND PEACE
Leo Tolstoy
93

Every action of theirs, that seems to them an act of their own free-will, is in the historical sense not free at all but is bound up with the whole course of history and preordained from all eternity.

The author believes that
☐ a. history repeats itself.
☐ b. free will is easily exercised.
☐ c. their every action was an act of free will.
☐ d. historical outcomes are predestined.

THE MYSTERY OF EDWIN DROOD
Charles Dickens
94

Rosa, having no relation that she knew of in the world, had, from the seventh year of her age, known no home but the Nuns' House, and no mother but Miss Twinkleton. Her remembrance of her own mother was of a pretty little creature like herself (not much older than herself it seemed to her), who had been brought home in her father's arms, drowned. The fatal accident had happened at a party of pleasure. Every fold and color in the pretty summer dress, and even the long wet hair, with scattered petals of ruined flowers still clinging to it, as the dead young figure, in its sad, sad beauty lay upon the bed, were fixed indelibly in Rosa's recollection. So were the wild despair and the subsequent bowed-down grief of her poor young father, who died broken-hearted on the first anniversary of that hard day.

After reading the passage the reader may assume that
☐ a. Rosa's mother died when she was seven.
☐ b. Rosa was bitter with her father after her mother's death.
☐ c. Rosa was morose.
☐ d. Rosa's remembrance of this experience would never leave her.

THE COUNTRY WIFE
William Wycherly
95

Alithea.

But why, sir, is marriage an enemy to you now? Because it robs you of your friend here? For you look upon a friend married as one gone into a monastery, that is, dead to the world.

Harcourt.

'Tis indeed because you marry him; I see, madam, you can guess my meaning. I do confess heartily and openly, I wish it were in my power to break the match; by heavens I would.

In this conversation, Harcourt implies that
- ☐ a. he likes Alithea, who has just arrived on the scene.
- ☐ b. marriage will change the relationship he and his friend have.
- ☐ c. he is opposed to all marriages, without exception.
- ☐ d. he is going to break up the match.

SISTER CARRIE
Theodore Dreiser
96

In 1889 Chicago had the peculiar qualifications of growth which made such adventuresome pilgrimages even on the part of young girls plausible. Its many and growing commercial opportunities gave it widespread fame, which made of it a giant magnet, drawing to itself, from all quarters, the hopeful and the hopeless—those who had their fortune yet to make and those whose fortunes and affairs had reached a disastrous climax elsewhere. It was a city of over 500,000, with the ambition, the daring, the activity of a metropolis of a million.

The writer suggests that in 1889, Chicago
- ☐ a. had a population growing faster than its industry.
- ☐ b. was heading towards disasters due to a very rapidly growing population.
- ☐ c. was the fastest growing city in the United States.
- ☐ d. attracted people with hope of financial opportunities greater than those actually existing.

CANDIDE
Voltaire
97

One day Cunegonde, walking near the castle in the little wood they called The Park, saw in the bushes Doctor Pangloss giving a lesson in experimental physics to her mother's chambermaid, a very pretty and very docile little brunette. Since Mademoiselle Cunegonde had much inclination for the sciences, she observed breathlessly the repeated experiments of which she was a witness; she clearly saw the Doctor's sufficient reason, the effects and the causes, and returned home all agitated, all pensive, all filled with the desire to be learned, thinking that she might well be the sufficient reason of young Candide, who might equally well be hers.

One may conclude from the passage that Dr. Pangloss
☐ a. is a very good physics instructor.
☐ b. has more than a professional interest in the chambermaid.
☐ c. is very learned in the art of logic.
☐ d. has developed in Cunegonde an acute interest in physics.

SISTER CARRIE
Theodore Dreiser
98

Hurstwood was still worthy, in a physical sense, of the affection his wife had once bestowed upon him, but in a social sense he fell short. With his regard died his power to be attentive to her, and this, to a woman, is much greater than outright crime toward another. Our self-love dictates our appreciation of the good or evil in another.

The writer suggests that Hurstwood
☐ a. failed socially as a husband.
☐ b. failed totally as a husband.
☐ c. was egotistical.
☐ d. was unfaithful.

61

THE BOSTONIANS
Henry James
99

"Now, I want you to tell me this," Basil Ransom said, leaning forward towards Verena, with his hands on his knees, and completely oblivious to his hostess. "Do you really believe all that pretty moonshine you talked last night? I could have listened to you for another hour; but I never heard such monstrous sentiments. I must protest—I must, as a calumniated, misrepresented man. Confess you meant it as a kind of *reductio ad absurdum*—a satire on Mrs. Farrinder?"

Basil Ransom's remarks indicate that
☐ a. he is an extremely "nosy" man.
☐ b. Verena had spoken unbelievably about Mrs. Farrinder.
☐ c. Verena likes to share her secrets with Basil.
☐ d. he enjoys gossip.

AMY FOSTER
Joseph Conrad
100

A sense of penetrating sadness, like that inspired by a grave strain of music, disengaged itself from the silence of the fields. The men we met walked past, slow, unsmiling, with downcast eyes, as if the melancholy of an over-burdened earth had weighted their feet, bowed their shoulders, borne down their glances.

"Yes," said the doctor to my remark, "one would think the earth is under a curse, since of all her children these that cling to her the closest are uncouth in body and as leaden of gait as if their very hearts were loaded with chains."

It may be inferred from the doctor's remark that he
☐ a. knows a great deal about the forces of nature.
☐ b. has little respect for people who make their livings from the land.
☐ c. has spent his entire life working the countryside.
☐ d. thinks being close to nature should be invigorating, not exhausting.

ACKNOWLEDGMENTS

Acknowledgment is gratefully made to the following publishers for permission to reprint the works of the many authors appearing in this series: To Harper & Row for permission to reprint passages by E. B. White, Richard Wright, Fletcher Knebel, Charles W. Bailey, Edward Streeter, and George Plimpton. To Random House for permission to reprint passages by William Styron, David Halberstam, Loren Eisely, Clifford Odets, and William Faulkner. To Harcourt Brace Jovanovich, Inc., for permission to reprint passages by C. F. Ramuz, George Orwell, Katherine Anne Porter, and Milovan Djilas. To Doubleday and Co., Inc., for permission to reprint passages by Melba Marlett, Hugh Downs, Leon Uris, Wyn Sargent, and J. F. Powers. To Little, Brown and Company for permission to reprint passages by Alastair Reid, Evelyn Waugh, Walter D. Edmonds, and Erich Maria Remarque. To Dodd, Mead & Company for permission to reprint passages by Cornelia Otis Skinner and Emily Kimbrough. To W. W. Norton & Company, Inc., for permission to reprint passages by Gordon S. Seagrove, M.D. To J. B. Lippincott Company for permission to reprint passages by Leslie A. Fiedler, Harper Lee, and Louis DeWohl. To Holt, Rinehart and Winston, Inc., for permission to reprint passages by Hannah Green and Philip Roth. To St. Martin's Press, Inc., for permission to reprint passages by James Herriot. To Charles Scribner's Sons for permission to reprint passages by F. Scott Fitzgerald and Dorothy Salisburgh Davis. To Century House, Inc., for permission to reprint passages by Percy Marks. To Scarecrow Press, Inc., for permission to reprint passages by Perry D. Westbrook. To Alfred A. Knopf, Inc., for permission to reprint passages by Elizabeth Brown and Katherine Mansfield. To Coward, McCann & Geoghegan, Inc., for permission to reprint passages by Bernard Kops. To The Viking Press, Inc., for permission to reprint passages by Patrich White. To Simon & Shuster, Inc., for permission to reprint passages by Mortimer Adler and P. G. Wodehouse. To Crown Publishers, Inc., for permission to reprint passages by Brainard Cheney. To The Dial Press for permission to reprint passages by Frank Yerby. To Farrar, Straus & Giroux, Inc., for permission to reprint passages by Shirley Jackson. To Houghton, Mifflin Company for permission to reprint passages by James Dickey and Ruth Benedict. To Oxford University Press, Inc., for permission to reprint passages by Aldo Leopold. To The John Day Company, Inc., for permission to reprint passages by Pearl S. Buck. To Berkley Publishing Corporation for permission to reprint passages by Theodore L. Thomas and Kate Wilhelm. To Pocket Books for permission to reprint passages by Benjamin Spock, M.D. To Rand McNally & Company for permission to reprint passages by Thor Heyerdahl. To The Viking Press, Inc., for permission to reprint passages by John Steinbeck and Muriel Spark. To E. P. Dutton Co., Inc., for permission to reprint passages by Dick Gregory and Alexander Solzhenitsyn. To The New American Library, Inc., for permission to reprint passages by Arthur Clarke. To Pitman Publishing Corp., for permission to reprint passages by John Holt. To World Publishing Company for permission to reprint passages by Kurt Steel. The story of the origin of the word "tantalize" is reprinted by permission from *Picturesque Word Origins*, copyright 1933 by G. & C. Merriam Co., publishers of the Merriam-Webster Dictionaries.

COMBINED ANSWER KEY AND RECORDING CHART

#	Ans	#	Ans	#	Ans	#	Ans	#	Ans
1	b	2	a	3	c	4	c	5	b
6	c	7	c	8	c	9	d	10	a
11	c	12	b	13	c	14	b	15	b
16	b	17	d	18	b	19	c	20	d
21	d	22	b	23	b	24	d	25	c

Score _____ %

#	Ans	#	Ans	#	Ans	#	Ans	#	Ans
26	b	27	c	28	b	29	c	30	d
31	c	32	b	33	b	34	d	35	b
36	c	37	d	38	b	39	b	40	a
41	c	42	c	43	b	44	a	45	c
46	b	47	b	48	c	49	c	50	b

Score _____ %

#	Ans	#	Ans	#	Ans	#	Ans	#	Ans
51	b	52	d	53	c	54	c	55	d
56	d	57	c	58	a	59	a	60	c
61	a	62	b	63	c	64	d	65	b
66	c	67	c	68	b	69	b	70	d
71	b	72	d	73	c	74	d	75	d

Score _____ %

#	Ans	#	Ans	#	Ans	#	Ans	#	Ans
76	d	77	c	78	a	79	c	80	d
81	b	82	a	83	b	84	c	85	a
86	a	87	b	88	b	89	b	90	c
91	c	92	a	93	d	94	d	95	b
96	d	97	a	98	b	99	b	100	d

Score _____ %